Fun All Seasons

Danielle Carroll

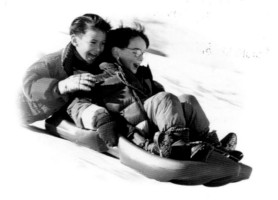

Rigby
A Harcourt Achieve Imprint

www.Rigby.com
1-800-531-5015

We can swim.

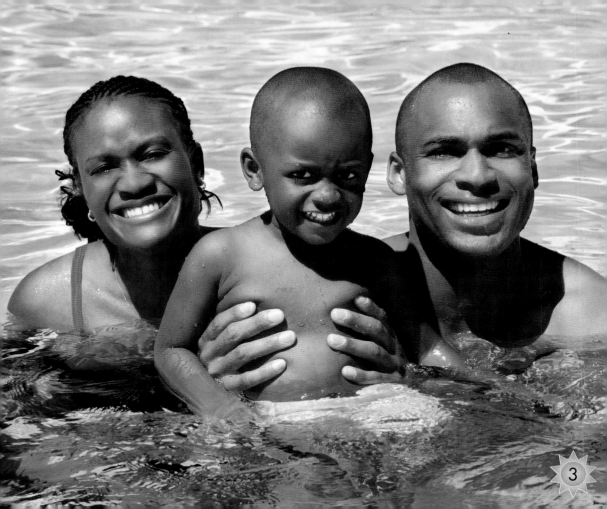

We can play.

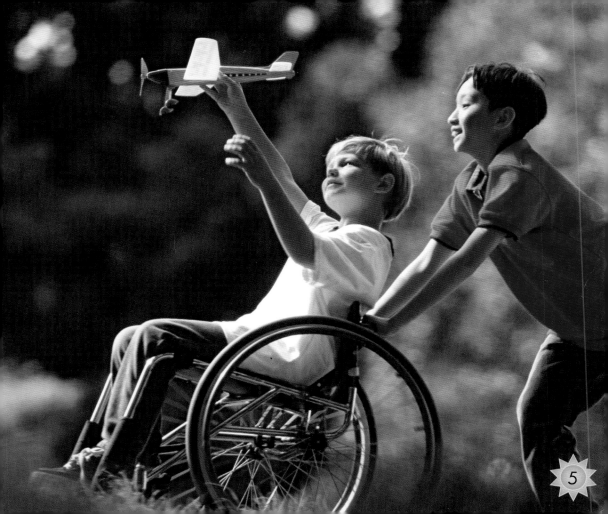

We can rake.

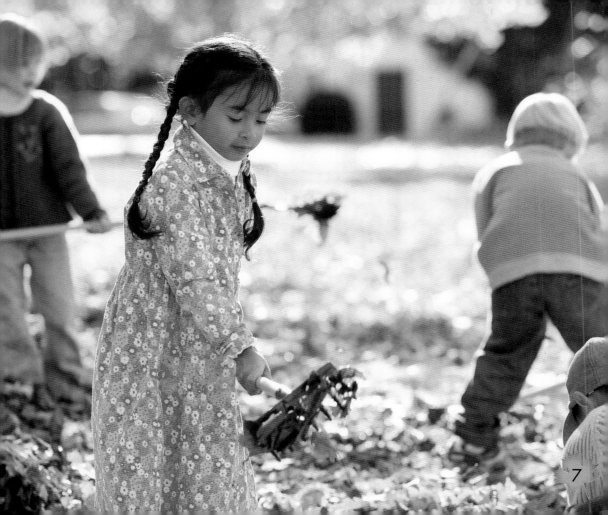

We can hop!

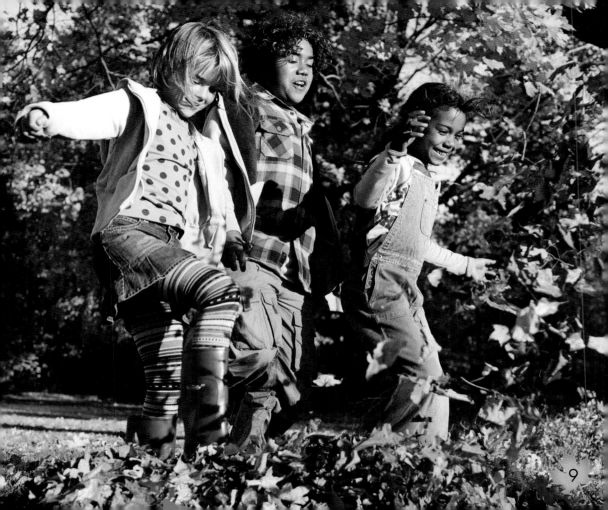

We can sled.

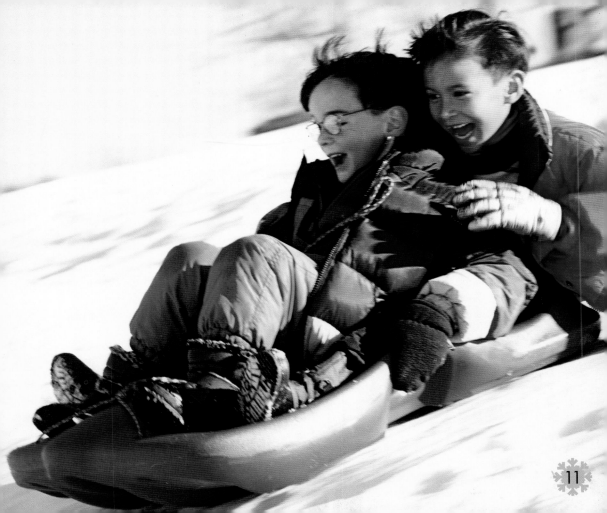

We can skate.

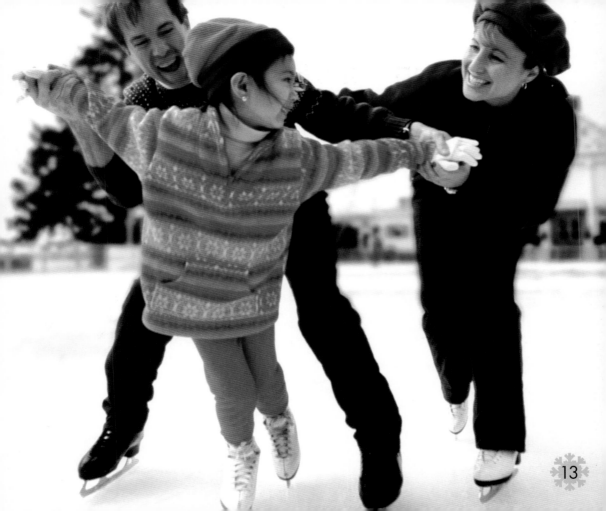

13

We can plant.

We can run!

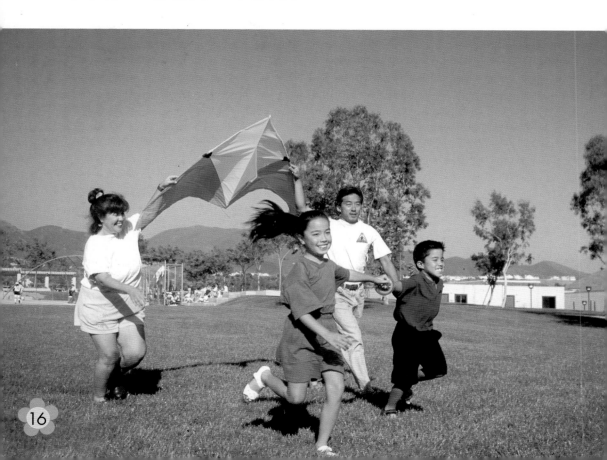

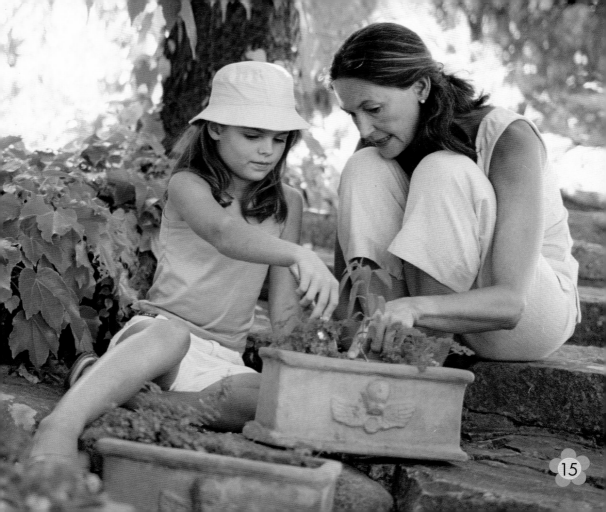